Crochet Scarves, Shawls & Ponchos

Step-By-Step Instructions for All of The Crochet Scarves, Shawls & Ponchos

DEDICATION

Contents

Any Season Asymmetrical Shawlette

What you will need:

- 1 hank fingering weight yarn, approx. 445 yds (shown here in Manos del Uruguay Alegria in the colorway A2545 Pewter), or more for larger shawl

- US E / 3.5 mm crochet hook

- scissors and needle

This pattern is written in U.S. crochet terms and abbreviations.

Finished size as written measures approx. 34.5" x 41" x 26.5", but is easily customization to the size you desire.

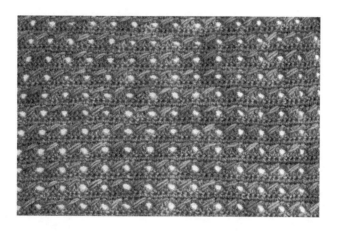

Ch 7.

Row 1: Work 1 sc in second ch from hook and each ch across, turn – 6 sts.

Row 2: Ch 1 (does not count as st here and throughout), work 1 sc in each st across, turn – 6 sts.

Row 3: Ch 3 (counts as dc here and throughout), skip next st, work 1 dc in each of the next 3 sts, work 1 dc back across the sts just made and into the skipped st, work 1 dc in last st, turn – 6 sts.

Row 4: Ch 1, work 2 sc in each of the next 3 sts, 1 sc in next, 2 sc in next, 1 sc in last, turn – 10 sts.

Row 5: Ch 3, *skip next st, work 1 dc in each of the next 3 sts, work 1 dc back across the sts just made and into the skipped st, repeat from *, work 1 dc in last st, turn – 10 sts.

Row 6: Ch 1, work 1 sc in each st across, turn – 10 sts.

Row 7: Ch 3, *skip next st, work 1 dc in each of the next 3 sts, work 1 dc back across the sts just made and into the skipped st, repeat from * across, work 1 dc in last st, turn – 10 sts.

Row 8: Ch 1, *work 2 sc in next st, 1 sc in next, rep from * 3 more times, work 1 sc in each of the remaining sts, turn – 14 sts.

Row 9: Ch 3, *skip next st, work 1 dc in each of the next 3 sts, work 1 dc back across the sts just made and into the skipped st, repeat from * across, work 1 dc in last st, turn – 14 sts.

Row 10: Ch 1, work 1 sc in each st across, turn – 14 sts.

Rows 11 through 110: Repeat Rows 7 through 10 until Row 110 or until desired length is reached, increasing by 4 sts with each repeat – 118 sts.

Pop of Color Shawl Crochet

MATERIALS:

Hook: I/9/5.5mm

Yarn: Cascade 220 Superwash Merino – 3 skeins doeskin heather (approx. 580 yards); 2 skeins sugar coral (approx. 310 yards)

Tools: Tapestry Needle & Scissors

ABBREVIATIONS:

st = stitch

ch = chain

sc=single crochet

dc=double crochet

sk=skip

sp=space

SPECIAL INFORMATION:

FINISHED SIZE: 65" wide, 40" long

Gauge: 12 dc x 8 rows = 4"

PATTERN:

Row 1: Using doeskin, make a magic ring. Ch 3 (counts as first dc here and throughout), 3 dc in ring, ch 2, 4 dc in ring, turn. Pull to tighten (8 dc)

Row 2: Ch 3, dc in the first st. Dc in each st to the ch-2 sp. (2 dc, ch 2, 2 dc) in ch-2 sp. Dc in each st to last st, 2 dc in the last st, turn. (14 dc)

Rows 3-39: Repeat row 2. At end of last row, fasten off.(Last row will have 236 dc)

Row 40: With sugar coral, ch 2 (counts as sc and ch-1), sc in the 2nd st. *ch 1, sk 1 st, sc in the next st*, repeat between * across to ch-2 sp, ch 1, (sc, ch 2, sc) in ch-2 sp, ch 1, sc into the first st after the ch-2 sp, rep between * across, to last st, ch 1, sc in last st, turn. (120 ch-1 sps, 122 sc)

Row 41: Ch 2, sc into the first ch-1 sp *ch 1, sk 1 sc, sc in the next ch-1 sp*, repeat between * across to ch-2 sp, ch 1, (sc, ch 2, sc) in ch-2 sp, ch 1, sc into the first ch-1 sp after the ch-2 sp, rep between * across ending with (sc, ch 1, sc) in last ch-2, turn. (122 ch-1 sps, 124 sc)

Row 42-49: Repeat row 41.

Fasten off and weave in all ends.

Sensational Crochet Shawl Pattern

Materials List

- 1 ball Red Heart Fashion Soft in Grey Heather (A)

- 1 ball Red Heart Fashion Soft in Camel (B)

- 1 ball Red Heart Fashion Heart Soft in Cream (C)

- 3.75 mm (US F-5) crochet hook

- Split lock stitch markers

- Yarn needle

Instructions:

Special Stitches:

Fan = (Dc, [ch 1, dc] twice) all in same indicated st or space

Stacked dc (stacked double crochet) = Sc in indicated st, insert hook behind leftmost vertical bar of sc just made and pull up a loop, yarn over and draw through 2 loops on hook.

V-st (V-stitch) = 2 dc in indicated st or space

Shawl

Using **A**, ch 4.

1. **Row 1 (right side):** Tr in 4th ch from hook and mark this ch, turn.

2. **Row 2:** Stacked dc in tr, 9 dc in ch-4 space, dc in unused loops of marked ch, remove marker, turn – 11 dc. Mark center dc, and move marker up to new center st as each row is completed.

3. **Row 3:** Stacked dc in first dc, 2 dc in same dc, dc in each dc to last dc before marked st, 2 dc in next dc, 3 dc in marked st, 2 dc in next dc, dc in each dc to last dc, 3 dc in last dc, turn – 19 dc

4. **Row 4:** Stacked dc in first dc, dc in same dc, ch 1, dc in next dc, [ch 1, skip next dc, dc in next dc] 3 times, ch 1, dc in next dc, ch 1, fan in next dc, [ch 1, dc in next dc] twice, [ch 1, skip next dc, dc in next dc] 3 times, ch 1, 2 dc in last dc, turn – 17 dc and 14 ch-1 spaces.

5. **Row 5:** Stacked dc in first dc, 2 dc in same dc, * dc in next dc, dc in next ch-1 space; repeat from * to center marker, 3 dc in marked st, dc in next ch-1 space, repeat from * to * to last 2 dc, dc in next dc, 3 dc in last dc, turn – 37 dc, 18 dc on either side of center marker

6. **Row 6:** Repeat Row 3 – 45 dc, 22 dc on either side of center marker

7. **Row 7:** Stacked dc in first dc, dc in same dc, ch 1, * dc in next dc, ch 1, skip next dc; repeat from * to last dc before marked dc, dc in next dc, ch 1, fan in marked dc, ch 1, repeat from * to * to last 2 dc, dc in next dc, ch 1, 2 dc in last dc, turn – 29 dc, 14 dc on either side of center marker

8. **Row 8:** Repeat Row 5 – 61 dc, 30 dc on either side of center marker.

9. **Row 9:** Stacked dc in first dc, dc in same dc, dc in each dc to last dc before marked st, 2 dc in next dc, 3 dc in marked st, 2 dc in next dc, dc in each dc to last dc, 2 dc in last dc, turn – 67 dc, 33 on either side of center marker.

10.   **Rows 10-27:** Repeat Rows 7-9 six more times – 199 dc, 99 dc on either side of center marker.

Change to **B**.

1. **Row 28:** Stacked dc in first dc, V-st in same dc * V-st in next dc, skip next dc; repeat from * to last dc before marker, V-st in next dc, (V-st, ch 1, V-st) in marked dc, V-st in next dc, repeat

from * to last dc, (V-st, dc) in last dc, turn — 52 V-sts on either side of center marker

2. **Row 29:** Stacked dc in first dc, ch 3, sc in space between first dc and first V-st, * ch 3, sc in space between V-sts, repeat from * to last dc, ch 3, sc in space between last V-st and last dc, ch 3, dc in last dc, turn — 53 ch-3 sps on either side of center marker

3. **Row 30:** Stacked dc in first dc, ch 1, sc in first ch-3 space, ch 1, * V-st in next ch-3 space, ch 1, sc in next ch-3 space, ch 1; repeat from * to marker, (dc, ch 1, dc) in marked sc, ch 1, sc in next ch-3 space, ch 1, repeat from * to * to end, dc in last dc, turn — 26 V-sts on either side of center marker.

4. **Row 31:** Stacked dc in first dc, ch 2, * dc in next ch-1 space, ch 1, dc in next ch-1 space, ch 2; repeat from * to marker, (dc, ch 1, dc) in marked ch-1 space, ch 2; repeat from * to * to end, dc in last dc, turn — 28 ch-2 spaces on either side of center marker

5. **Row 32:** Stacked dc in first dc, fan in each ch-2 space to marker, fan in marked space, fan in each ch-2 space to end, dc in last dc, turn — 28 fans on either side of center marker

6. **Row 33:** Stacked dc in first dc, ch 1, * dc in next ch-1 space, ch 1, dc in next ch-1 space, ch 2, repeat from * to last ch-1 space before marker, dc in next ch-1 space, ch 1, skip marked dc, dc in next ch-1 space, ch 2, repeat from * to * to last 2 ch-1 spaces (last fan), (dc, ch 1) in each of last 2 ch-1 spaces, dc in last dc, turn – 28 ch-2 spaces on either side of center marker

7. **Row 34:** Stacked dc in first dc, dc in first ch-1 space, ch 1, * sc in next ch-1 space, ch 1, V-st in ch-2 space, ch 1; repeat from * to marker, (dc, ch 1, dc) in marked ch-1 space, ch 1, V-st in next ch-2 space, ch 1, repeat from * to * to last 2 ch-1 spaces, sc in next ch-1 space, ch 1, dc in last ch-1 space, dc in last dc, turn – 28 V-sts on either side of center marker

8. **Row 35:** Stacked dc in first dc, ch 2, dc in first ch-1 space, ch 1, * dc in next ch-1 space, ch 2, dc in next ch-1 space, ch 1, repeat from * to marker, (dc, ch 2, dc) in marked space, ch 1, repeat from * to * to last ch 1 space, dc in last ch-1 space, ch 2, dc in last dc, turn – 29 ch-2 spaces on either side of center marker

9. **Rows 36-47:** Repeat Rows 32-35 3 more times – 32 ch-2 spaces on either side of center marker

10.   **Row 48:** Repeat Row 32 – 32 fans on either side of center marker

Change to **C**.

1. **Row 49:** Stacked dc in first dc, * [dc in next dc, dc in next ch-1 space] twice, dc in next dc, ch 1, skip (dc, ch 1), sc in next dc, ch 1, skip (ch 1, dc), repeat from * to last fan, [dc in next dc, dc in next ch-1 space] twice, dc in each of last 2 dc, turn – 83 dc on either side of marker.

2. **Row 50:** Stacked dc in first dc, ch 1, dc in same dc, * skip next dc, sc in next dc, ch 3, skip next dc, sc in next dc, fan in next sc, repeat from * to last 6 dc, skip next dc, sc in next dc, ch 3, skip next dc, sc in next dc, (dc, ch 1, dc) in last dc, turn – 16 fans on either side of center marker

3. **Row 51:** Stacked dc in first dc, ch 3, sc in next ch-3 space, * ch 3, sc in next ch space; repeat from * to last ch-1 space, skip last ch-1 space, ch 3, dc in last dc, turn – 49 ch-3 spaces on either side of center marker

4. **Row 52:** Stacked dc in first dc, ch 3, * sc in next ch-3 space, ch 3; repeat from * to marker, (dc, ch 1, dc) in marked sc, ch 3, repeat from * to * to end, dc in last dc, turn – 50 ch-3 spaces on either side of center marker

5. **Row 53:** Stacked dc in first dc, ch 3, * sc in next ch space, ch 3, sc in next ch space, fan in next ch space; repeat from * to last 2 spaces, [sc in next ch space, ch 3] twice, dc in last dc, turn – 16 fans on either side of center marker

6. **Rows 54 and 55:** Stacked dc in first dc, ch 3, * sc in next ch space, ch 3; repeat from * to end, dc in last dc, turn – 53 ch-3 spaces on either side of center marker at end of Row 55.

7. **Row 56:** Repeat Row 52 – 54 ch-3 spaces on either side of center marker.

8. **Row 57:** Stacked dc in first dc, ch 3, * sc in next ch-3 space, ch 3, sc in next ch-3 space, fan in next ch-3 space; repeat from * to marker, fan in marked st, fan in next ch-3 space, ch 3, repeat from * to * to last 2 ch-3 spaces, [sc in next ch-3 space, ch 3], twice, dc in last dc, turn – 18 fans on either side of center marker

9. **Row 58-61:** Repeat Row 54 4 times — 58 ch-3 spaces on either side of center marker at end of Row 61

10. **Row 62:** Stacked dc in first dc, ch 3, * sc in next ch-3 space, ch 3, sc in next ch-3 space, fan in next ch-3 space; repeat from * to last ch-3 space before marker, sc in next ch-3 space, marker, fan in marked st, ch 3, sc in next ch-3 space, fan in next ch-3 space, repeat from * to * to last 2 ch-3 spaces, [sc in next ch-3 space, ch 3], twice, dc in last dc, turn — 18 fans on either side of center marker — 19 fans on either side of marker

11. **Row 63 and 64:** Repeat Row 54 and 55 — 61 ch-3 spaces on either side of marker at end of Row 64

12. **Row 65:** Stacked dc in first dc, ch 3, * sc in next ch-3 space, ch 3; repeat from * to marker, (dc, ch 1, dc) in marked sc, ch 3, repeat from * to * to end, dc in last dc, turn — 62 ch-3 spaces on either side of marker

13. **Rows 66 and 67:** Repeat Rows 54 and 55 — 63 ch-3 spaces on either side of marker at end of Row 67

14.   **Row 68:** Stacked dc in first dc, ch 1, * sc in next ch-3 space, fan in next ch-3 space, repeat from * to last ch-3 space, sc in last ch-3 space, ch 1, dc in last dc, turn – 31 fans on either side of marker.

Edging

1. **Round 1:** Ch 1, sc in each st and ch-1 space around, join with slip st in first sc. Fasten off.

Finishing

1. Weave in all loose ends. Lightly wet block or steam block to measurements.

Vintage Lace Popcorn Shawl

Crochet Hook: F/5 or 3.75 mm hook

Yarn Weight: (2) Fine (23-26 stitches to 4 inches)

Crochet Gauge: 17 dc and 9 rows = 4 ins [10 cm]

Finished Size: Approx 8 x 60 ins [20.5 x 152.5 cm].

Materials List

- Patons® Lace (85 g /3 oz; 455 m/498 yds) 33008 (Vintage) 1 ball

- Size 3.75 mm (U.S. F or 5) crochet hook or size needed to obtain tension.

Pattern

Ch 50. (See Chart below).

CHART

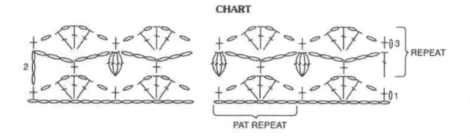

1. **1st row**: (WS). 1 sc in 2nd ch from hook. *Ch 1. Miss next 3 ch. [(1 dc. Ch 1) twice. 1 dc] all in next ch. Ch 1. Miss next 3 ch. 1 sc in next ch. Rep from * to end of ch. Turn.

2. **2nd row:** Ch 6 (counts as dc and ch 3). Miss next dc. 1 sc in next dc. *Ch 3. 4 dc in next sc. Drop loop from hook, insert hook in first dc of 4 dc group and pull dropped loop through. Ch 1 – Popcorn made. Ch 3. Miss next dc. 1 sc in next dc. Rep from * across, ending with 1 dc in last sc. Turn.

3. **3rd row:** Ch 1. 1 sc in first dc. *Ch 1. [(1 dc. Ch 1) twice. 1 dc] all in next sc. Ch 1.** 1 sc in top of next Popcorn. Rep from * 4

times more, then from * to ** once. 1 sc in 3rd ch of ch 6. Turn.

4. Rep last 2 rows for pat until Scarf measures approx 60 ins [152.5 cm], ending on a 3rd row. Fasten off.

5. **Edging**: With RS facing, join yarn with sl st to bottom right corner. Ch 1. Work 1 row of sc evenly along side edge. Fasten off. Rep for other side.

Pineapple Lace Shawl Crochet Pattern

Difficulty Level: Intermediate

Crochet Hook: J/10 or 6 mm hook

Yarn Weight: (4) Medium Weight/Worsted Weight and Aran (16-20 stitches to 4 inches)

Crochet Gauge: In pattern stitch, 23 sts and 3 rows = 4"/10 cm. Exact gauge is not critical for this project.

Finished Size: approximately 48"/122 cm wide x 24"/61 cm long

Materials List

- Yarn: Caron International's Simply Soft Eco (80% Acrylic, 20% NatureSpun™ Polyester): 10 oz #0034 Black

- Crochet Hook: One size US J-10 (6 mm) crochet hook, or size to obtain gauge.

- Yarn needle

How to Crochet the Pineapple Lace Shawl

Instructions

Ch 10; taking care not to twist ch, join with slip st in first ch to form a ring.

1. **Row 1:** Ch 4 (counts as first tr), work 22 tr in ring, turn—23 tr.

2. **Row 2:** Beg-trCl in first tr, *ch 3, skip next tr, trCl in next tr; repeat from * across, working last trCl in top of turning ch, turn—12 clusters.

3. **Row 3:** Beg-trCl in first trCl, *ch 2, tr in next ch-3 space, ch 2, trCl in next trCl; repeat from * across, turn—12 clusters and 11 tr.

4. **Row 4:** Beg-trCl in first trCl, *ch 3, tr in next tr, ch 3, trCl in next trCl; repeat from * across, turn.

5. **Row 5:** Beg-trCl in first trCl, *ch 4, tr in next tr, ch 4, trCl in next trCl; repeat from * across, turn.

6. **Row 6:** Beg-trCl in first trCl, *ch 5, tr in next tr, ch 5, trCl in next trCl; repeat from * across, turn.

7. **Row 7:** Beg-trCl shell in first trCl, *ch 4, tr in next tr, ch 4, trCl shell in next trCl; repeat from * across, turn—12 shells and 11 tr.

8. **Row 8:** Beg-trCl in first trCl, ch 5, trCl in next trCl, *ch 3, tr in next tr, ch 3, trCl in next trCl, ch 5, trCl in next trCl; repeat from * across, turn—24 clusters and 11 tr.

9. **Row 9:** Beg-trCl in first trCl, ch 9, trCl in next trCl, *ch 3, tr in next tr, ch 3, trCl in next trCl, ch 9, trCl in next trCl; repeat from * across, turn.

10. **Row 10:** Beg-trCl in first trCl, ch 5, sc in 5th ch of next ch-9 space, picot, ch 5, trCl in next trCl, *picot, trCl in next trCl, ch 5, sc in 5th ch of next ch-9 space, picot, ch 5, trCl in next trCl; repeat from * across, turn—24 clusters.

11. **Row 11:** Beg-trCl in first trCl, ch 5, 6 tr in next picot, ch 5, *trCl shell in next picot, ch 5, 6 tr in next picot, ch 5; repeat from * across to last trCl, trCl in last trCl, turn—11 shells, 2 clusters and 12 6-tr groups.

12. **Row 12:** Beg-trCl in first trCl, ch 5, sc in next tr, [ch 6, sc in next tr] 5 times (beginning of pineapple), ch 5, *trCl shell in ch-3 space of next trCl shell, ch 5, sc in next tr, [ch 6, sc in next tr] 5 times, ch 5; repeat from * across to last trCl, trCl in last trCl, turn—11 shells, 2 clusters, and 12 pineapple beginnings.

13. **Row 13:** Beg-trCl in first trCl, ch 6, [sc in next ch-6 space, ch 6] 5 times, *trCl shell in ch-3 space of next trCl shell, ch 6, [sc in

next ch-6 space, ch 6] 5 times; repeat from * across to last trCl, trCl in last trCl, turn.

14. **Row 14:** Beg-trCl in first trCl, ch 6, skip next ch-6 space, [sc in next ch-6 space of pineapple, ch 6] 4 times, *trCl shell in ch-3 space of next trCl shell, ch 6, skip next ch-6 space, [sc in next ch-6 space of pineapple, ch 6] 4 times; repeat from * across to last trCl, trCl in last trCl, turn.

15.   **Row 15 (trCl shell increase row):** Beg-trCl shell in first trCl, ch 6, skip next ch-6 space, [sc in next ch-6 space of pineapple, ch 6] 3 times, *trCl shell-inc in ch-3 space of next trCl shell, ch 6, skip next ch-6 space, [sc in next ch-6 space of pineapple, ch 6] 3 times; repeat from * across to last trCl, trCl shell in last trCl, turn—11 shell increases, 2 shells, and 12 pineapples.

16. **Row 16:** Beg-trCl in first trCl, ch 3, sc in next ch-3 space, ch 3, trCl in next trCl, ch 6, skip next ch-6 space, [sc in next ch-6 space of pineapple, ch 6] twice, *[trCl in next trCl, ch 3, sc in next ch-3 space, ch 3] twice, trCl in next trCl, ch 6, skip next ch-6 space, [sc in next ch-6 space of pineapple, ch 6] twice;

repeat from * across to last shell, trCl in next trCl, ch 3, sc in next ch-3 space, ch 3, trCl in last trCl, turn—37 clusters, and 12 pineapples.

17.   **Row 17:** Beg-trCl in first trCl, [ch 3, sc in next ch-3 space] twice, ch 3, trCl in next trCl, ch 3, sc in next ch-6 space, ch 3, (sc, ch 3, sc) in next ch-6 space (pineapple point), ch 3, sc in next ch-6 space, ch 3, **trCl in next trCl, *[ch 3, sc in next ch-3 space] twice, ch 3, trCl in next trCl; repeat from * once more, ch 3, sc in next ch-6 space, ch 3, (sc, ch 3, sc) in next ch-6 space (pineapple point), ch 3, sc in next ch-6 space, ch 3; repeat from ** to last 2 trCl, trCl in next trCl, [ch 3, sc in next ch-3 space] twice, ch 3, trCl in last trCl, turn.

18.   **Row 18:** Ch 5, sc in next ch-space, *ch 3, sc in next ch-space; repeat from * across skipping all trCl to last trCl, ch 3, slip st in last trCl, turn.

19.   Do not fasten off.

Edging

Note: Work edging around entire shawl as follows:

1. **Row 1:** Ch 5, sc in next ch-3 space, *ch 3, sc in next ch-space; repeat from * across, ch 3, sc in same (last) ch-space again (for corner); pivot to work along top edge, **ch 3, sc in end of next row; repeat from ** across working (sc, ch 3, sc) in center of beginning ring; ch 3, join with slip st in 2nd ch of beginning ch-5, do not turn.

2. **Row 2:** Beg-trCl in same st as join; *ch 3, slip st in next ch-3 space, ch 3, trCl in next ch-3 space; repeat from * across to opposite top corner, ending with ch 3, sl st in corner ch-space; working along top edge, work 3 sc in each ch-space across; join with slip st in Beg-trCl. Fasten off.

Finishing

Using yarn needle, weave in ends. If desired, block lightly.

Abbreviations

Ch: chain

Sc: single crochet

slip st: slip stitch

Picot sl st in st, Ch 6, sl st in top of last st made.

Tr: Treble stitch—Yarn over twice, insert hook in indicated stitch and draw up a loop (4 loops on hook), yarn over and draw through 2 loops on hook (3 loops on hook), yarn over and draw through 2 loops on hook (2 loops on hook), yarn over and draw through 2 loops on hook (1 loop on hook)

Beg-trCl: Beginning treble cluster—Ch 4, yarn over twice, insert hook in indicated stitch and draw up a loop, [yarn over and draw through 2 loops on hook] twice (2 loops on hook); yarn over twice, insert hook in same stitch and draw up a loop, [yarn over and draw through 2 loops on hook] twice (3 loops on hook); yarn over and draw through all 3 loops on hook.

trCl: Treble cluster—Yarn over twice, insert hook in indicated stitch and draw up a loop, [yarn over and draw through 2 loops on hook] twice (2 loops on hook); *yarn over twice, insert hook in same stitch and draw up a loop, [yarn over and draw through 2 loops on hook] twice; repeat from * once more; yarn over and draw through all 4 loops on hook.

29

Beg-trCl shell: Beginning treble cluster shell— (Beg-trCl, ch 3, trCl) in indicated stitch.

trCl shell: Treble cluster shell— (trCl, ch 3, trCl) in indicated stitch.

trCl shell-inc: Treble cluster shell increase— ([trCl, ch 3] twice, trCl) in indicated stitch.

Perfectly Paris Poncho

Crochet Hook: I/9 or 5.5 mm hook

Yarn Weight: (4) Medium Weight/Worsted Weight and Aran (16-20 stitches to 4 inches)

Materials

Bernat® Berella 4

Bernat® Super Value

Bernat® Satin

Size 5.5 mm (U.S. I or 9) crochet hook or size needed to obtain gauge.

Assembly Diagram

Photographed garment made with Bernat Super Value (Grey)

Size XS/M

390 g (13.75 oz)/685 m (760 yds)

Size L/2XL

485 g (17 oz)/850 m (945 yds)

Size 3/5XL

585 g (20.5 oz)/1025 m (1140 yds)

GAUGE:

12 dc and 7 rows = 4 ins [10 cm].

SIZES:

To fit bust measurement

Extra-Small/Medium

28 - 38 ins [71 - 96.5 cm]

Large/2 Extra-Large

40 - 50" [101.5 - 127"]

3 Extra-Large/5 Extra-Large

52 - 62" [132 - 157.5"]

Finished measurement from neck edge to point

Extra-Small/Medium

18¾ ins [47.5 cm]

Large/2 Extra-Large

21½" [54.5"]

3 Extra-Large/5 Extra-Large

25¼" [64"]

Instructions

The instructions are written for smallest size. If changes are necessary for larger sizes the instructions will be written thus ( ).

Note: Turning ch 2 does not count as a stitch.

When working tr push stitch to RS of work.

When working Bobble, push Bobble to RS of work.

Make 2 pieces alike.

Ch 41 (47-53).

1st row: (WS). 1 hdc in 3rd ch from hook (counts as 1 hdc). 1 hdc in each ch to end of ch. 39 (45-51) hdc.

2nd row: Ch 3 (counts as dc). Miss first hdc. *Dcfp around next hdc. 1 dc in each of next 2 hdc. (Yoh and draw up a loop. Yoh and draw through 2 loops on hook) 4 times in next hdc. Yoh and draw through all loops on hook – Bobble made. 1 dc in each of next 2 hdc. Rep from * to last 2 sts. Dcfp around next hdc. 1 dc in last hdc. Turn.

3rd row: Ch 2. 1 hdc in first dc. *Dcbp around next st. 1 hdc in each of next 5 sts. Rep from * to last 2 sts. Dcbp around next st. 1 hdc in last dc. Turn.

4th row: Ch 1. 1 sc in first st. *1 tr in next st. 1 sc in next sc. Rep from * to end of row.

5th row: Ch 2. 1 hdc in each st to end of row.

Rep rows 2 to 5 for pat until work from beg measures approx 27 (29-31) ins [68.5 (73.5-78.5) cm], ending with 3rd or 5th row. Fasten off.

Finishing

Pin garment pieces to measurements and cover with damp cloth leaving cloth to dry.

Sew 2 pieces tog as shown in Diagram.

Top edging: Join yarn with sl st at any seam at neck edge.

1st rnd: Ch 1. 1 sc in same sp as sl st. Work 83 sc around neck edge. Join with sl st to first sc.

2nd rnd: (Eyelet rnd). Ch 2. 1 hdc in same sp as last sl st. *(Ch 1. Miss next sc. 1 hdc in next sc. Rep from *to last sc. Ch 1. Miss last sc. Join with sl st to first hdc.

3rd rnd: Working from left to right instead of right to left as usual, work 1 reverse sc in each st around. Join with sl st to first sc. Fasten off.

Bottom edging: Join yarn with sl st to any corner at bottom.

1st rnd: Ch 1. 3 sc in same sp as last sl st. Work 120 (132-144) sc along bottom edge to next corner. 1 sc in point.

Work 120 (132-144) sc to next corner. Join with sl st to first sc.

2nd rnd: Ch 2. 1 hdc in same sp as last sl st. *Ch 1. Miss next sc. 1 hdc in next sc. Rep from * to last sc (having 1 hdc. Ch 1. 1 hdc in each corner sc). Ch 1. Miss last sc. Join with sl st to first hdc.

3rd rnd: Working from left to right instead of right to left as usual, work 1 reverse sc in each st around. Join with sl st to first sc. Fasten off.

Drawstring: Make a chain 40 ins [101.5 cm] long.

1st row: Sl st in 2nd ch from hook. 1 sl st in each ch to end of ch. Fasten off.

Beg at center front, thread Drawstring through eyelets at neck edge.

Simple Crochet Poncho

Supplies:

• Lion Brand Touch of Alpaca Bonus Bundle (Weight: 4/medium – 415 yds, 7 oz)

– Taupe (124-123) – 6 (7, 7, 8) skeins [approx. 1140, (1250, 1390, 1490) g]

• Tapestry needle

• Size J (6.0 mm) crochet hook

• Stitch markers or safety pins

Sizes:

S/M – fits bust: 35"

M/L – fits bust: 39"

L/XL – fits bust: 43"

XL/2X – fits bust: 47"

Sample is a M/L pictured on a 5'8" model with a 38" bust. Poncho has a generous 42" of ease.

Main body of poncho when laying flat (excluding collar and sleeves) measures:

S/M – 38.5" wide x 25.75" long

M/L – 40.5" wide x 26.5" long

L/XL – 42.5" wide x 27.25" long

XL/2X – 44.5" wide x 28" long

Gauge:

Main Poncho:

4.5 horizontal clusters (sc, hdc, dc) = 4"

5.5 vertical clusters (11 rows worked in pattern) = 4"

Ribbing:

14 hdc = 4"

10 rows = 4"

Abbreviations and Glossary (US Terms):

ch(s) – chain(s)

dc – double crochet

hdc – half double crochet

hdcblo – half double crochet through the back loop only

PM – place marker

rep – repeat

]RS – right side

sc – single crochet

sk – skip

st(s) – stitch(es)

tch – turning chain

WS – wrong side

Overall Pattern + Sizing Notes:

• Poncho is constructed from five rectangles. Left front and back of poncho are worked at the same time, as are the right front and back.

PONCHO FRONTS AND BACKS

Notes:

• Right front and back of poncho and left front and back are worked identically.

• A horizontal "cluster" = 1 sc, 1 hdc, 1 dc. Vertically, 2 rows equal a complete cluster.

Make 2.

Foundation Row: Ch 177 (183, 189, 195). [177 (183, 189, 195)]

Row 1 (RS): Sk 2 chs (counts as 1 sc), work [hdc, dc] in next ch, *sk 2 chs, work [sc, hdc, dc] in next ch; rep from * until 3 chs remain, sk 2 chs, sc in last ch; turn. [58 (60, 62, 64) horizontal clusters]

Row 2 (WS): Ch 1 (counts as 1 sc), work [hdc, dc] in first st, *sk [1 dc, 1 hdc], work [sc, hdc, dc] in next sc; rep from * until 3 sts remain, sk [1 dc, 1 hdc], sc in top of tch; turn.

Rep Row 2 another 48 (50, 52, 54) more times for a total of 50 (52, 54, 56) rows. [This will look like 25 (26, 27, 28) vertical clusters.] End with a WS row. Do not fasten off.

Indent for Neckline

Notes:

Front:

Row 1 (RS): Ch 1 (counts as 1 sc), work [hdc, dc] in first st, *sk [1 dc, 1 hdc], work [sc, hdc, dc] in next sc; rep from * 24 (25, 25, 26) times, sk [1 dc, 1 hdc], sc in next sc; turn. [26 (27, 27, 28) horizontal clusters]

From here, all remaining rows are worked over these 26 (27, 27, 28) horizontal clusters.

Row 2 (WS): Ch 1 (counts as 1 sc), work [hdc, dc] in first st, *sk [1 dc, 1 hdc], work [sc, hdc, dc] in next sc; rep from * until 3 sts remain, sk [1 dc, 1 hdc], sc in top of tch; turn. [26 (27, 27, 28) horizontal clusters]

Rep Row 2 another 7 (8, 9, 10) more times for a total of 59 (62, 65, 68) rows from Foundation Row. [This will look like 29.5 (31, 32.5, 34) vertical clusters.] Fasten off leaving a 35" tail.

Back:

With RS facing, sk 4 (4, 6, 6) horizontal clusters to create neck space. Attach yarn in sc of 5th (5th, 7th, 7th) unused sc from "Front" indent edge.

Row 1 (RS): Ch 1 (counts as 1 sc), work [hdc, dc] in first st, *sk [1 dc, 1 hdc], work [sc, hdc, dc] in next sc; rep from * until 3 sts remain, sk [1 dc, 1 hdc], sc in top of tch; turn. [27 (28, 28, 29) horizontal clusters]

From here, all remaining rows are worked over these 27 (28, 28, 29) horizontal clusters.

Row 2 (WS): Ch 1 (counts as 1 sc), work [hdc, dc] in first st, *sk [1 dc, 1 hdc], work [sc, hdc, dc] in next sc; rep from * until 3 sts remain, sk [1 dc, 1 hdc], sc in top of tch; turn. [27 (28, 28, 29) horizontal clusters]

Rep Row 2 another 7 (8, 9, 10) more times for a total of 59 (62, 65, 68) rows from Foundation Row. [This will look like 29.5 (31, 32.5, 34) vertical clusters.] Fasten off leaving a 35" tail.

Final rectangle (including the additional rows for the neckline) should measure approx. 51.75 (53.25, 54.75, 56.25)" x 19.25 (20.25, 21.25, 22.25)".

SLEEVES

Notes:

• Sleeve rectangles are worked lengthwise. To shorten or lengthen sleeve, adjust number of chains in Foundation Row.

• For a tighter sleeve, work fewer total rows. For a looser sleeve, work more rows. In both cases, take care to work an even number of rows total. Note that adjusting sleeve in this way will impact the amount of room you want to leave open for armhole when you seam main poncho pieces together.

• Ribbed look is created by working through the back loop only of each hdc stitch. This is the loop that's farthest away from you, regardless of whether the WS or RS of work is facing you.

• Ch 2 at beginning of row does not count as a hdc.

Make 2.

Foundation Row: Ch 39 (40, 41, 39). [39 (40, 41, 39)]

Row 1 (RS):]Sk 2 chs, hdc in each ch to end of row. [37 (38, 39, 37)]

Row 2 (WS): Ch 2, hdcblo in each hdc to end of row. [37 (38, 39, 37)]

Rep Row 2 another 18 (20, 22, 22) more times for a total of 20 (22, 24, 24) rows. [This will look like 10 (11, 12, 12) ridges of ribbing.] Fasten off leaving a 25" tail.

COLLAR

Notes:

• Collar rectangle is worked horizontally. To shorten or lengthen height of collar, adjust number of chains in Foundation Row.

• Like with sleeves, the ribbed look is created by working through the back loop only of each hdc stitch. This is the loop that's farthest away from you, regardless of whether the WS or RS of work is facing you.

• Ch 2 at beginning of row does not count as a hdc.

Make 1.

Foundation Row: Ch 36 (38, 40, 42). [36 (38, 40, 42)]

Row 1 (RS): Sk 2 chs, hdc in each ch to end of row. [34 (36, 38, 40)]

Row 2 (WS): Ch 2, hdcblo in each hdc to end of row. [34 (36, 38, 40)]

Rep Row 2 another 49 (53, 66, 70) more times for a total of 51 (55, 68, 72) rows. [This will look like 25.5 (27.5, 34, 36) ridges of ribbing.] Fasten off leaving a 30" tail.

FINISHING

Shades of Indigo Poncho

MATERIALS:

2 skeins Lion Brand Jeans in Vintage or approx. 492yds/450m of another worsted weight, cat. 4 yarn for Color A

2 skeins Lion Brand Jeans in Brand New or approx. 492yds/450m of another worsted weight, cat. 4 yarn for Color B

2 skeins Lion Brand Jeans in Stonewash or approx. 492yds/450m of another worsted weight, cat. 4 yarn for Color C

1 skein Lion Brand Jeans in Top Stitch or approx. 492yds/450m of another worsted weight, cat. 4 yarn for Color D

1 skein Lion Brand Jeans in Top Stitch or approx. 246yds/225m of another worsted weight, cat. 4 yarn for Color E

2 skeins Lion Brand Jeans in Faded or approx. 492yds/450m of another worsted weight, cat. 4 yarn for Color F

2 skeins Lion Brand Jeans in Stovepipe or approx. 492yds/450m of another worsted weight, cat. 4 yarn for Color G

Size US J-10 (6mm) crochet hook

Tapestry needle

FINISHED SIZE:

Width: 48"/123cm

Length from shoulder to bottom edge: 30"/76cm

GAUGE:

13.5 sts + 10 rows = 4"/10cm in half double crochet

ABBREVIATIONS:

All Two of Wands patterns are written in standard US terms

Ch - Chain

Hdc - Half double crochet

MB - Make bobble

Rep - Repeat

RS - Right side

St(s) - Stitch(es)

STITCH EXPLANATION:

Make Bobble (MB) – Yarn over, insert hook into stitch to be worked, draw up a loop, yarn over, pull through first 2 loops on hook (2 loops on hook remain). Yarn over, insert hook into same stitch, draw up a loop, yarn over, pull through first 2 loops on hook (3 loops on hook remain). Repeat 3 more times for a total of 5 sts worked into the same st (6 loops on hook). Yarn over and pull through all loops on hook.

Note: Pattern is worked in several rectangles that are seamed together to form poncho. The diagram indicates the placement of each piece. The ch 2 at the beginning of each row does not count as a stitch. It is imperative to check gauge and maintain an even tension throughout to ensure pieces fit together.

Piece 1: 48"/122cm long x 6"/15cm wide

Using color A, ch 164.

Row 1: Starting in 3rd ch from hook, hdc across row. (162 sts)

Rows 2-15: Ch 2 (does not count as stitch here and throughout), hdc across row.

Piece 2: 54"/137cm long x 6"/15cm wide

Using color B, ch 184.

Row 1: Starting in 3rd ch from hook, hdc across row. (182 sts)

Rows 2-15: Ch 2, hdc across row.

Piece 3: 26"/66cm long x 12"/30.5cm wide

Using color C, ch 90.

Row 1: Starting in 3rd ch from hook, hdc across row. (88 sts)

Rows 2-30: Ch 2, hdc across row.

Piece 4: 16"/41cm long x 12"/30.5cm wide

Note: Work all bobbles in color E. To change color, work the last yarn over of the previous stitch in the new color. On rows with bobbles/color changes, join color E at the first bobble and carry it along while not in use, cutting it off after the last bobble – to carry along, lay the unused color E on top of the previous row and work over it with color D.

Using color D, ch 56.

Row 1 (RS): Starting in 3rd ch from hook, hdc across row. (54 sts)

Rows 2 and 3: Ch 2, hdc across row.

Row 4: Ch 2, hdc 9, MB, (hdc 16, MB) twice, hdc remaining 10.

Rows 5-9: Ch 2, hdc across row.

Row 10: Ch 2, (hdc 17, MB) twice, hdc remaining 18.

Rows 11-15: Ch 2, hdc across row.

Row 16: Ch 2, hdc 9, MB, (hdc 16, MB) twice, hdc remaining 10.

Row 17-21: Ch 2, hdc across row.

Row 22: Ch 2, (hdc 17, MB) twice, hdc remaining 18.

Rows 23-27: Ch 2, hdc across row.

Row 28: Ch 2, hdc 9, MB, (hdc 16, MB) twice, hdc remaining 10.

Rows 29 and 30: Ch 2, hdc across row.

Piece 5: 10"/25cm long x 6"/15cm wide

Using color E, ch 36.

Row 1: Starting in 3rd ch from hook, hdc across row. (34 sts)

Rows 2-15: Ch 2, hdc across row.

Piece 6: 28"/71cm long x 8"/20cm wide

Using color F, ch 96.

Row 1: Starting in 3rd ch from hook, hdc across row. (94 sts)

Rows 2-20: Ch 2, hdc across row.

Piece 7: 24"/61cm long x 18"/46cm wide

Using color G, ch 84.

Row 1: Starting in 3rd ch from hook, hdc across row. (82 sts)

Rows 2-45: Ch 2, hdc across row.

Piece 8: 22"/56cm long x 10"/25cm wide

Note: Work all bobbles in color E. To change color, work the last yarn over of the previous stitch in the new color. On rows with bobbles/color changes, join color E at the first bobble and carry it along while not in use, cutting it off after the last bobble – to carry along, lay the unused color E on top of the previous row and work over it with color D.

Using color D, ch 76.

Row 1 (RS): Starting in 3rd ch from hook, hdc across row. (74 sts)

Rows 2 and 3: Ch 2, hdc across row.

Row 4: Ch 2, hdc 9, MB, (hdc 17, MB) three times, hdc remaining 10.

Rows 5-9: Ch 2, hdc across row.

Row 10: Ch 2, hdc 18, MB, (hdc 17, MB) twice, hdc remaining 19.

Rows 11-15: Ch 2, hdc across row.

Row 16: Ch 2, hdc 9, MB, (hdc 17, MB) three times, hdc remaining 10.

Row 17-21: Ch 2, hdc across row.

Row 22: Ch 2, hdc 18, MB, (hdc 17, MB) twice, hdc remaining 19.

Rows 23-25: Ch 2, hdc across row.

Piece 9: 24"/61cm long x 8"/20cm wide

Using color C, ch 84.

Row 1: Starting in 3rd ch from hook, hdc across row. (82 sts)

Rows 2-20: Ch 2, hdc across row.

Piece 10: 16"/41cm long x 6"/15cm wide

Using color B, ch 56.

Row 1: Starting in 3rd ch from hook, hdc across row. (54 sts)

Rows 2-15: Ch 2, hdc across row.

Piece 11: 18"/46cm long x 14"/35.5cm wide

Using color A, ch 62.

Row 1: Starting in 3rd ch from hook, hdc across row. (60 sts)

Rows 2-35: Ch 2, hdc across row.

Piece 12: 16"/41cm long x 10"/25cm wide

Using color E, ch 56.

Row 1: Starting in 3rd ch from hook, hdc across row. (54 sts)

Rows 2-25: Ch 2, hdc across row.

Piece 13: 16"/41cm long x 8"/20cm wide

Using color F, ch 56.

Row 1: Starting in 3rd ch from hook, hdc across row. (54 sts)

Rows 2-20: Ch 2, hdc across row.

Construction:

Block each piece to specified measurements. Lay pieces out as indicated by diagram. Seam pieces together, leaving the center front, indicated by the thick black line on diagram, open and un- seamed approx. 30"/76cm from bottom edge. Secure and weave in all ends.

Belt:

Using color F, ch 212. Starting in 3rd ch from hook, hdc across row.

Fold poncho at shoulder line and lay flat with back side facing up. Lay belt across the back and poke the ends through to the other side through spaces in the stitches, roughly at the waist line but slightly wider. Turn poncho over so that front is facing up. Poke ends up through corresponding spaces on either front piece so that belt is laced through all pieces and can be tied in front.

To make tassels, cut forty 12"/30.5cm lengths and four 18"/46cm lengths of color D. Divide the 12"/ 30.5cm lengths into two groups of 20. Tie each bundle at the middle point with one of the 18"/ 46cm lengths. Fold each bundle in half so that the tie is at the tip of the loop created with the fold. Tie crosswise around each folded bundle about 1/2"/1.25cm below top of fold with remaining 18"/ 46cm lengths. Wrap the tails of the ties around and around the bundles and then thread them inside and down the middle of the bundles with a tapestry needle. Tie the tops of the tassels onto the ends of the belt and knot to secure. Thread the tails inside and down the middle of the tassels using a tapestry needle. Trim tassels to desired length.

Sweater Poncho

Supplies:

—Lion Brand ZZ Twist yarn (Weight: 4/Medium — 3.5oz, 246 yds)

Color: Peacock — 5 (6, 6, 7, 7, 7, 8) skeins (approx. 460, 520, 550, 610, 650, 710, 750 g)

—Size I 5.5 mm hook

—Tapestry needle

—Measuring tape or ruler

Sizes:

XS, S, M, L, Xl, XXL, XXXL

Abbreviations (US terms):

ch — chain

blo — back loop only

dc — double crochet

sk — skip

st(s) — stitch(es)

t – turn

Skill Level: Level 2 Easy

Notes:

-This sweater/poncho fits very oversized. For reference, model is 5'5" tall with a 38" bust and wearing the Twist Swancho in size Medium.

-If you'd like a fit as pictured on me, follow your usual size. If you're between sizes, please size down.

-Sizing listed in the pattern will be in X-Small with Small, Medium, Large, Xl, 2X, and 3X listed in parenthesis such as 36 "(41, 46, 51, 56, 61, 66)" whereas Ch 36 for size XS, 41 for size S, 46 for size M, 51 for size L, 56 for size XL, 61 for size 2X and 66 for size 3X. When only one number is given, it applies to all sizes. To follow pattern more easily, circle/highlight all numbers pertaining to your size before beginning.

-Pattern is worked by first making the back panel and front panel then seaming them up to create the swancho shape. Assembly instructions will be the same for all sizes.

-Ch 2 does not count as a stitch.

Gauge:

12 sts x 11 rows in Dc = 4"

Dimensions:

XS – 19 x 26"

S – 20 x 28"

M – 20 x 30"

L – 21 x 32"

XL – 21 x 34"

XXL – 22 x 36"

XXXL – 22 x 38"

Instructions:

Twist Swancho

Back panel

Row 1: Ch 82 (87, 87, 92, 92, 97, 97), Dc in 3rd Ch from hook, Dc to end, Ch 2, t (80, 85, 85, 90, 90, 95, 95)

Row 2: BLO Dc in each st, Ch 2, turn (80, 85, 85, 90, 90, 95, 95)

Repeat Row 2 until you reach the correct length for your size as follows:

X-Small: Work to Row 63

Small: Work to Row 68

Medium: Work to Row 73

Large: Work to Row 78

XL: Work to Row 83

2XL: Work to Row 88

3XL: Work to Row 93

Finish off yarn.

Front Panel

Row 1: Ch 82 (87, 87, 92, 92, 97, 97), Dc in 3rd Ch from hook, Dc to end, Ch 2, t (80, 85, 85, 90, 90, 95, 95)

Row 2: BLO Dc in each st, Ch 2, turn (80, 85, 85, 90, 90, 95, 95)

Repeat Row 2 until you reach the correct length for your size as follows:

X-Small: Work to Row 75

Small: Work to Row 80

Medium: Work to Row 85

Large: Work to Row 90

XL: Work to Row 95

2XL: Work to Row 100

3XL: Work to Row 105

Finish off yarn.

Twist:

Lay back piece down flat, lengthwise (in a landscape orientation.

Lay front piece on top. Twist center of front piece as pictured.

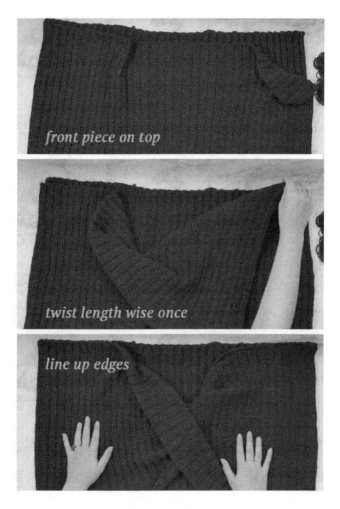

front piece on top

twist length wise once

line up edges

Line up edges of front piece to back piece.

Use stitch markers to mark where your shoulder seams will end and open for the neckline. Do this by measuring 9.5 (10, 11, 11.5, 12.5, 13, 13.5) inches inward (toward the center) from either side. Be sure to mark both front and back pieces together. Double check that your markings match by counting rows.

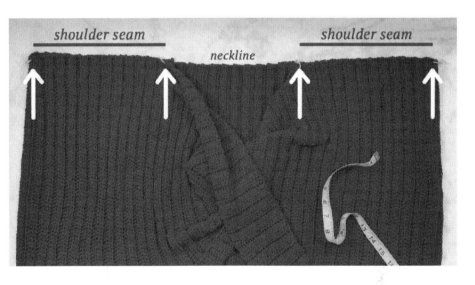

Use stitch marker to mark where your side seams will end and open for the armholes. Do this by measuring 9.5 (10, 11, 11.5, 12.5, 13, 13.5) inches from the shoulder seam or top edge of the side seam (shorter sides of your panels. Be sure to mark both front and back pieces together. Double check that your markings match by counting stitches.

Seams:

With a spare piece of yarn (cut to about 3x the length of the area where your side seam will be), use a mattress stitch to seam up the sides of your cardigan and the shoulder seams.

Repeat side seam and shoulder seam on the other side. Weave all ends.

Crochet Tunic Poncho

Supplies:

Yarn

Is a light fingering, 3 ply yarn in the lace category, but since I used a bigger hook then recommended, you can use also a 4 ply, fingering yarn as long as you get to the gauge.

1 skein has 100 grams and 450 meters

Crochet hook

3.5 mm (E US size)

tapestry needle

scissors

Approximate how much yarn do you need

S – 350 grams/1470 m/1602 yds

M – 380 grams / 1580 m/ 1720 yds

L – 400 grams / 1680 m/ 1830 yds

XL – 430 grams / 1800 m / 1960 yds

XXL – 460 grams / 1930 m / 21010 yds

About the stitches you will have to now

The square is worked using 3 different basic stitches

half double crochet (hdc)

double crochet (dc)

Triple crochet (trc)

We will also use

chain (ch)

slip stitch (sl st)

Other abbreviations used in the pattern

st (s) – Stitch (s)

Bellow you can find a crochet chart with the first rounds of the square

Gauge

8 rows (measured in diagonal) – 10 cm (4")

17 dc – 10 cm (4 ")

And with all these details being said, we are ready to start making this beautiful Poncho-Tunic.

Instructions:

Start with a magic ring.

Ch 3 and make 11 dc inside the ring. Sl st with the 3rd st of the starting chain.

Round 1

ch3, [1 dc in the next 3 sts, ch 4, 1 dc in the same st with the previous dc,] repeat this section to the end of the round. Finish the round with ch 4 and sl st with the 3rd st of the starting chain.

Round 2

*Tip: starting with this round you can count the ch 2 as a first hdc, but I recommend not to, because it will be easier to join with a 1st hdc than with the second st of the starting chain.

ch 2, go back to the previous ch 4, and make 3 hdc in the ch 4 space, 1 dc in the next 2 sts, 1 trc in the next 2, ch 4 [3 hdc in the ch 4 space, 1 dc in the next 2 sts, 1 trc in the next 2].

Repeat the section between [ ] to the end of the round, ending the round with ch 4 and sl st with the first hdc.

Round 3

Ch 2, 2 hdc in the previous ch 4 space, 1 hdc in the next st (on the top of the first hdc from the previous round), 1 dc in the next 3 sts, 1 trc in the next 3 [ch 4, 2 hdc in the ch 4 space, 1 hdc in the next, 1 dc in the next 3 sts, 1 trc in the next 3]

Repeat the section between [ ] to the end of the round, ending the round with ch 4 and sl st with first hdc.

Round 4

Ch 2, 3 hdc in the previous ch 4 space, 1 hdc in the next st, 1 dc in the next 4 sts, 1 trc in the next 4 sts, [ch 4, 3 hdc in the ch 4 space, 1 hdc in next, 1 dc in next 4 sts, 1 trc in next 4 sts].

Repeat the section between [ ] to the end of the round ending the round with ch 4 and sl st with first hdc.

Round 5

Ch 2, 3 hdc in the previous ch 4 space, 1 hdc in next 2, 1 dc in next 5 sts, 1 trc in next 5, [ch 4, 3 hdc in the ch 4 space, 1 hdc in next 2 sts, 1 dc in next 5 sts, 1 trc in next 5 sts].

Repeat the section between [ ] to the end of the round ending the round with ch 4 and sl st with first hdc.

For example on round 6 we will have 6 hdc, 6 dc and 6 trc and always 3 hdc in the ch 4 space.

We will continue to add with each round, one more stitch of each kind until we will get to the end of the square.

For each size you will have in total for a square:

S – 23 rounds (23 sts of each kind on one side of the square)

M – 25 rounds (25 sts of each kind on one side of the square)

L – 27 rounds (27 sts of each kind on one side of the square)

XL – 29 rounds (29 sts of each kind on one side of the square)

XXL – 31 rounds (31 sts of each kind on one side of the square)

After finishing one square you will have to make 4. After that, depending on what kind of yarn you are using, you might need to block them before assembling.

Assembling

Fold 2 squares in half and lay them with one corner next to each other, to form a triangle between them. These 2 squares will be the sleeves.

In the space between them put the 2 other squares, one over the other. These 2 will be the front side and the back side.

Then sew the squares together.

Asymmetric Crochet Chevron Cowl

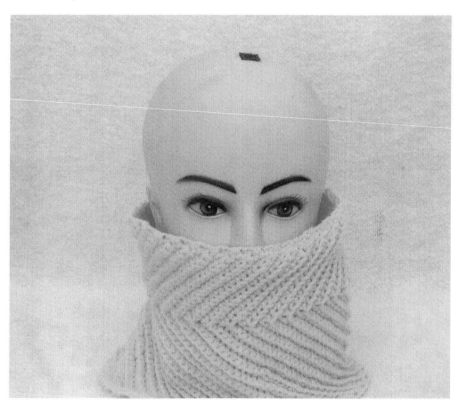

MEASUREMENT

Toddler – 17 inches circumference, 6 inches height

Child – 20 inches circumference, 7 inches height

Teen/Small Adult – 23 inches circumference, 8 inches height

Large Adult – 27 inches circumference, 9 inches height

MATERIALS:

5.5 mm crochet hook

Worsted weight yarn – 100-150g

Stitch markers (Optional)

Yarn needle

DIFFICULTY:

Beginner

GAUGE :

18 stitches /12 rows = 10 cm/4 inches in pattern stitch

STITCH GUIDE (US VERSION)

Ch: Chain

Sc: Single Crochet

Slst: Slip stitch

Scblo: Single Crochet in back loops only

Sc2tog: Single Crochet two together

PATTERN NOTES

Ch 1 at the beginning of the rows does not count as a stitch

The cowl is worked flat and then seamed.

PATTERN INSTRUCTIONS:

Ch 35(41,47,53)

Row 1: Sc into the second chain from the hook, Sc into the next 11(13,15,17) chains, 3 Sc in the next stitch, Sc in the remaining

21(25,29,33) stitches

Row 2: Ch 1, turn. Sc2tog in the back loops only. Scblo in the next 20(24,28,32) stitches . 3 Scblo in the next stitch stitch, Scblo in the next 11(13,15,17) stitches, finish row with Sc2tog in the back loops only.

Row 3: Ch 1, turn. Sc2tog in the back loops only. Scblo in the next 11(13,15,17) stitches . 3 Scblo in the next stitch stitch, Scblo in the next 20(24,28,32)stitches, finish row with Sc2tog in the back loops only.

Rows 4-51(60,69,78): keep alternating rows 2 and 3.

FINISHING

Ch 1, turn. Working into back loops only Slst to the starting chains to close the cowl, Sc3tog the 3 Sc in the same stitch, do not finish the

Sc3tog, Slst to the corresponding starting chain,continue Slst till the cowl is closed. Ch 1 and cut yarn.

Or sew the beginning and end together. Make sure to sew the 3 Sc in the same stitch to the corresponding starting chain. Sew your cowl to the end. Ch 1 and cut yarn.

Weave in all ends.

UK VERSION

SIZES

Toddler (Child, Teen/Small Adult, Large Adult)

MEASUREMENT

Toddler – 17 inches circumference, 6 inches height

Child – 20 inches circumference, 7 inches height

Teen/Small Adult – 23 inches circumference, 8 inches height

Large Adult – 27 inches circumference, 9 inches height

MATERIALS:

5.5 mm crochet hook

Worsted weight yarn – 100-150g

Stitch markers (Optional)

Yarn needle

DIFFICULTY:

Beginner

GAUGE :

18 stitches /12 rows = 10 cm/4 inches in pattern stitch

STITCH GUIDE (UK VERSION)

Ch: Chain

Dc: Double Crochet

Slst: Slip stitch

Dcblo: Double Crochet in back loops only

Dc2tog: Double Crochet two together

PATTERN NOTES

Ch 1 at the beginning of the rows does not count as a stitch

The cowl is worked flat and then seamed.

PATTERN INSTRUCTIONS:

Ch 35(41,47,53)

Row 1: Dc into the second chain from the hook, Dc into the next 11(13,15,17) chains, 3 Dc in the next stitch, Dc in the remaining 21(25,29,33) stitches

Row 2: Ch 1, turn. Dc2tog in the back loops only. Dcblo in the next 20(24,28,32) stitches . 3 Dcblo in the next stitch stitch, Dcblo in the next 11(13,15,17) stitches, finish row with Dc2tog in the back loops only.

Row 3: Ch 1, turn. Dc2tog in the back loops only. Dcblo in the next 11(13,15,17) stitches . 3 Dcblo in the next stitch stitch, Dcblo in the next 20(24,28,32)stitches, finish row with Dc2tog in the back loops only.

Rows 4-51(60,69,78): keep alternating rows 2 and 3.

FINISHING

Working into back loops only Slst to the starting chains to close the cowl, Dc3tog the 3 Dc in the same stitch, do not finish the Dc3tog, Slst to the corresponding starting chain,continue Slst till the cowl is closed. Ch 1 and cut yarn.

Or sew the beginning and end together. Make sure to sew the 3 Dc in the same stitch to the corresponding starting chain. Sew your cowl to the end. Ch 1 and cut yarn.

Weave in all ends.

Made in the USA
Columbia, SC
06 July 2024

38215616R00048